Starry Arms

Counting by Fives

Special thanks to our advisers for their expertise:

Stuart Farm, M.Ed., Mathematics Lecturer
University of North Dakota, Grand Forks

Susan Kesselring, M.A., Literacy Educator
Rosemount-Apple Valley-Eagan (Minnesota) School District

by Michael Dahl
illustrated by Todd Ouren

PICTURE WINDOW BOOKS
Minneapolis, Minnesota

Managing Editor: Catherine Neitge
Creative Director: Terri Foley
Art Director: Keith Griffin
Editor: Christianne Jones
Designer: Todd Ouren
Page production: Picture Window Books
The illustrations in this book were prepared digitally.

Picture Window Books
5115 Excelsior Boulevard
Suite 232
Minneapolis, MN 55416
877-845-8392
www.picturewindowbooks.com

Printed in the United States of America.

Library of Congress Cataloging-in-Publication Data
Dahl, Michael.
Starry arms : counting by fives / written by Michael Dahl ;
illustrated by Todd Ouren.
p. cm. — (Know your numbers)
ISBN 1-4048-0947-3 (hardcover)
1. Counting—Juvenile literature. 2. Multiplication—Juvenile
literature. 3. Starfishes—Juvenile literature. I. Ouren, Todd,
ill. II. Title.

QA113.D353 2004
513.2'11—dc22   2004018429

Look what's swishing in the sandy surf.

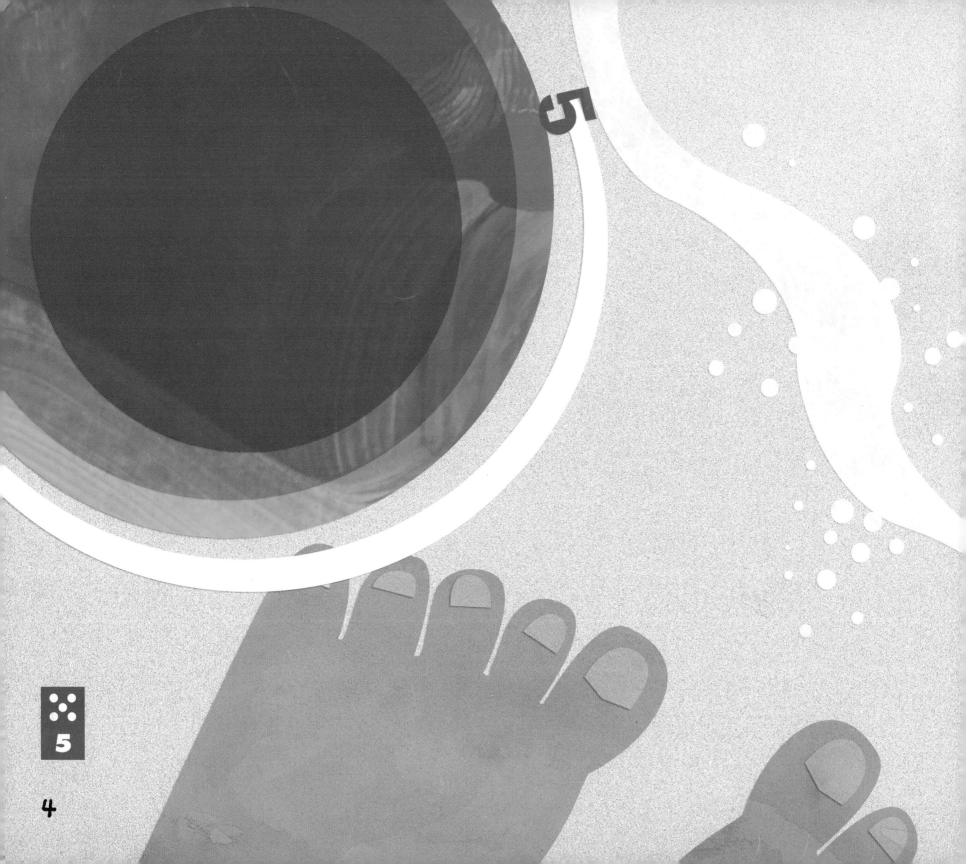

5

A starfish lies upon the sand.

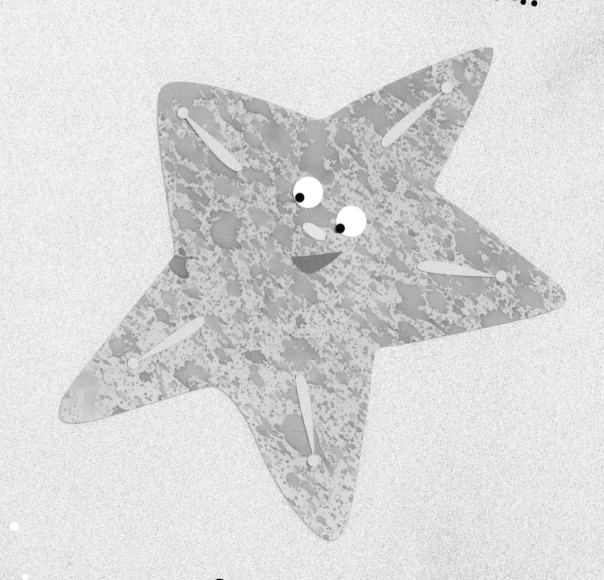

FIVE starfish arms.

Starfish touch without a hand.

TEN starfish arms.

Starfish dance and starfish twirl.

FIFTEEN starfish arms.

Starfish crawl and starfish curl.

5 10 15 20

TWENTY starfish arms.

Starfish cling to slippery stones.

5 | 10 | 15 | 20 | 25

12

TWENTY-FIVE starfish arms.

Starfish creep through fishy bones.

5 10 15 20 25 30

THIRTY starfish arms.

Starfish swim through wild waves.

5 10 15 20 25 30 35

THIRTY-FIVE starfish arms.

Starfish climb through coral caves.

FORTY starfish arms.

19

Starfish rest on soft sandbars.

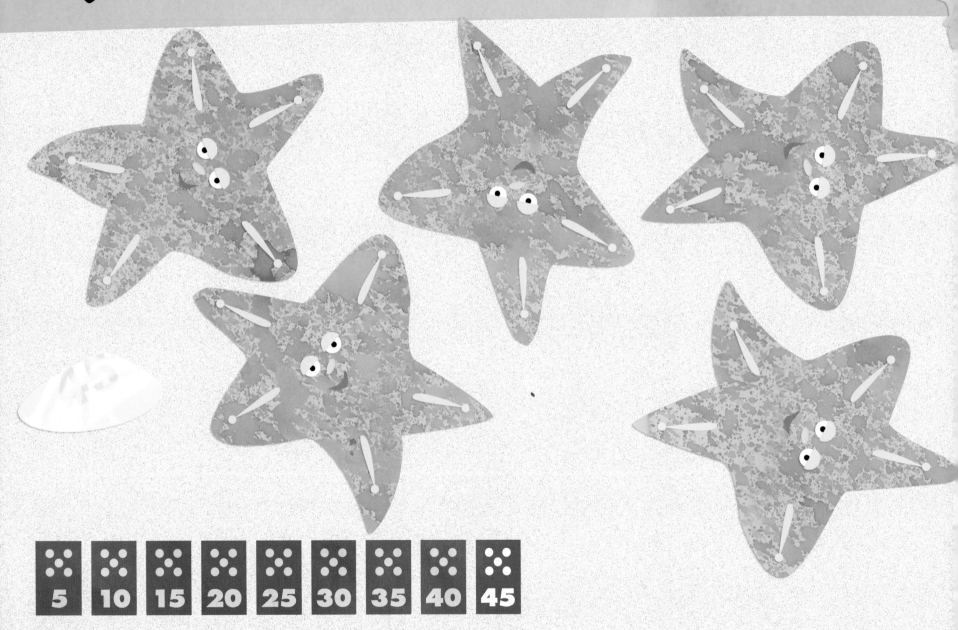

FORTY-FIVE starfish arms.

Starfish sleep beneath the stars.

5 10 15 20 25 30 35 40 45 50

22

FIFTY starfish arms.

Fun Facts

Starfish don't have brains.

If the arm of a starfish is cut off, it will grow back.

Starfish are not really fish. They are creatures called echinoderms, which means "prickly skin."

Starfish cannot hear or smell anything.

Starfish are not always orange. They are also pink, purple, and yellow.

On the Web

FactHound offers a safe, fun way to find Web sites related to this book. All of the sites on FactHound have been researched by our staff. *www.facthound.com*

1. Visit the FactHound home page.

2. Enter a search word related to this book, or type in this special code: 1404809473

3. Click on the FETCH IT button.

Your trusty FactHound will fetch the best sites for you!

Find the Numbers

Now you have finished reading the story, but a surprise still awaits you. Hidden in each picture is a multiple of 5 from 5 to 50. Can you find them all?

5 –on the bucket near the handle

10 –beside the clam's eyes

15 –between the seaweed on the right

20 –on the third starfish

25 –on the seaweed

30 –on the bottom left skeleton

35 –on the splash

40 –on the coral between the seaweed

45 –on the white shell

50 –on the top right star

Look for all of the books in the Know Your Numbers series:

Downhill Fun
A Counting Book About Winter

Eggs and Legs
Counting By Twos

Footprints in the Snow
Counting By Twos

From the Garden
A Counting Book About Growing Food

Hands Down
Counting By Fives

Lots of Ladybugs!
Counting By Fives

On the Launch Pad
A Counting Book About Rockets

One Big Building
A Counting Book About Construction

One Checkered Flag
A Counting Book About Racing

One Giant Splash
A Counting Book About the Ocean

Pie for Piglets
Counting By Twos

Starry Arms
Counting By Fives